Dedication

To the resilient spirit of democracy, which - even in its darkest of days - finds a way to renew itself through honorable representatives of the people.

This tale is respectfully dedicated to all those past and present who have worked to protect the virtues of open debate, consensus building, and good faith participation in civic affairs.

Though the path is seldom easy, leaders like Lord Speaker Micah Jones remind us what real progress looks like - achieved step by step, person to person, through compassion and unity rather than division.

It is their steady guidance that keeps the promise of self-governance burning bright for generations to come.

Prologue

It had been a decade since the last transition of power in the Upper House, an unprecedented period of stability that brought much prosperity to the realm. However, all knew that Lady Shireen's stewardship—blessed as it was—

must come to an end someday. When news arrived of her sudden illness, a wave of uncertainty passed through Cameral. The great lords and ladies of the Upper House came together at Storm's End to choose her successor in a session behind closed doors.

Two candidates quickly emerged as favorites—Lord Renly, next in line through inheritance but lacking experience, and Ser Davos, the venerable small councilor renowned for his service. After a marathon debate stretching late into the night, votes were cast. By a razor-thin margin, Renly Baratheon was named the new Voice of the Upper House. Down in the city, ripples of unease were felt in the halls of the Lower House. For their esteemed Lord Speaker, Stannis, was brother to the late Lady Shireen.

In accordance with tradition, his position was forfeit now that his kin no longer held the highest office. But none could have predicted what turmoil would soon grip the chamber in the power vacuum left behind.

Stannis himself took the change stiffly but with dignity, collecting his affairs to return north to Storm's End. As he departed the City of Sails for the last time, whispers hinted at his displeasure over theUpper House result. But protecting stability was now in younger hands.

In his last act, Stannis adjourned the Lower House until a new speaker could be chosen. Little did any foresee how arduous that task would be.

For within those stone walls lay dormant ambitions that would soon be awoken, ideologies about to clash, and all the makings of a crisis to test the realm's strength of character as never before. Our story is about to begin...

The halls of the Lower House of Cameral were abuzz with activity as honored lords and ladies from across the realm made their way inside the grand chamber. It had been three weeks since the unexpected change in leadership in the Upper House had caused the previous Lord Speaker to lose his seat.

The other members of the Lower House had spent the intervening weeks in a state of disorder and chaos, with no one able to take charge and guide the debates and proceedings. Factions formed and battled for supremacy, each seeking to promote their own candidate for the vacant speaker position.

Accusations and insults were traded frequently as tempers flared in the power vacuum.

Finally, the assembled lords and ladies took their seats in preparation to choose a new leader.

Dozens of names had been proposed during the campaigning period, but four candidates emerged as the favorites after weeks of negotiations, alliances, and politicking behind closed doors.

Lady Elara Tyrell
Lord Devon Forrester
Lord Ser Devos Seaworth
Lord Micah Jones

Lady Elara Tyrell - As the daughter of a wealthy and influential Duke, Elara was well-connected within the aristocracy. However, she had gained a reputation over the years as arrogant and entitled. While she promised to use her family's resources to restore stability, many feared she would not respect the independence of the Lower House.

Lord Devon Forrester - A veteran member who had held numerous leadership roles over three decades, Devon was seen as the safest pair of hands. But at 57 years old, some felt he was too entrenched in old ways of thinking and lacked the dynamism needed. His support mainly came from the other elderly conservatives.

Ser Davos Seaworth - As a former naval captain turned small councilor, Davos brought a commoner's touch that many liked. But only recently elevated to lordship and the Lower House, some questioned if an outsider understood the intricacies and traditions expected of the Speaker.

Lord Micah Jones - While Micah had gained respect for his intellect and reform agenda, his relative youth of 35 counted against him. Some dismissed him as too green and inexperienced. But his breakthrough speeches during the campaign energized others who felt it was time for new blood and a less partisan approach.

His populist message
resonated more than
expected.

Each was given an opportunity to address the chamber and make their case for why they were most fit to restore order and lead the Lower House. All brought qualifications but also weaknesses that were hotly debated in the crucial weeks before the consequential vote.

When it was Micah Jones' turn to speak, a hush fell over the room. Though still a relatively young lord at only 35 years of age, Jones had already proven himself a formidable debater and strategist during his decade of service.

He spoke passionately about his vision for bringing civility and cooperation back to their deliberations. Where the other candidates emphasized their experience or familial connections, Jones focused on outlining specific reforms aimed at preventing future deadlocks.

After the final candidate finished, an hour was dedicated to further discussions before the vote. When the time came, the chamber held its collective breath as the tellers tallied the results. In a surprising upset, Micah Jones had secured a narrow majority.

DEBATE

Wild cheers erupted from his supporters at the announcement while stunned faces greeted the result amongst his opponents. As per tradition, the newly elected Lord Speaker was carried around the chamber on the shoulders of his allies, beaming proudly at what lay ahead.

Over the following weeks, Lord Speaker Jones got straight to work implementing the changes he had promised. New rules of decorum were established to curb unruly behavior and promote respectful debate.

The scheduling of bills and proposals was reformed to prevent partisan obstructionism. And an independent ethics committee was formed to investigate any accusations of improper conduct by members.

✗ Improper conducts *****

Under Jones' steady leadership, the Lower House began to regain its rhythm and function as the realm expected. Controversial issues that had languished for months were finally brought to votes.

Mutual understanding and cooperation gradually replaced the bitterness and gridlock of the prior speakership. Most impressive was Jones' ability to unite disparate factions and broker compromises, a skill which had previously alluded his predecessors.

Mutual understanding***

Cooperation**

As our story ends half a year later, the reforms instituted by Lord Speaker Micah Jones have borne fruit. Civility and productivity are the new norms within the Lower House of Cameral once more.

Civility

&

Though far from perfect, the restoration of order and consensus under Jones' dynamic speakership has been nothing short of remarkable. His rise from relative obscurity to the heights of power serves as an inspiration that one person truly can make a positive difference.

The realm is no doubt grateful this young leader stepped up in their hour of need.

THE END

www.ingramcontent.com/pod-product-compliance
Lightning Source LLC
Chambersburg PA
CBHW040236240726
48664CB00001B/148